Ca'Myiah's Land

By FaraNita Dunbar, LIMHP

Illustrations created or adapted by Thalia Dunbar

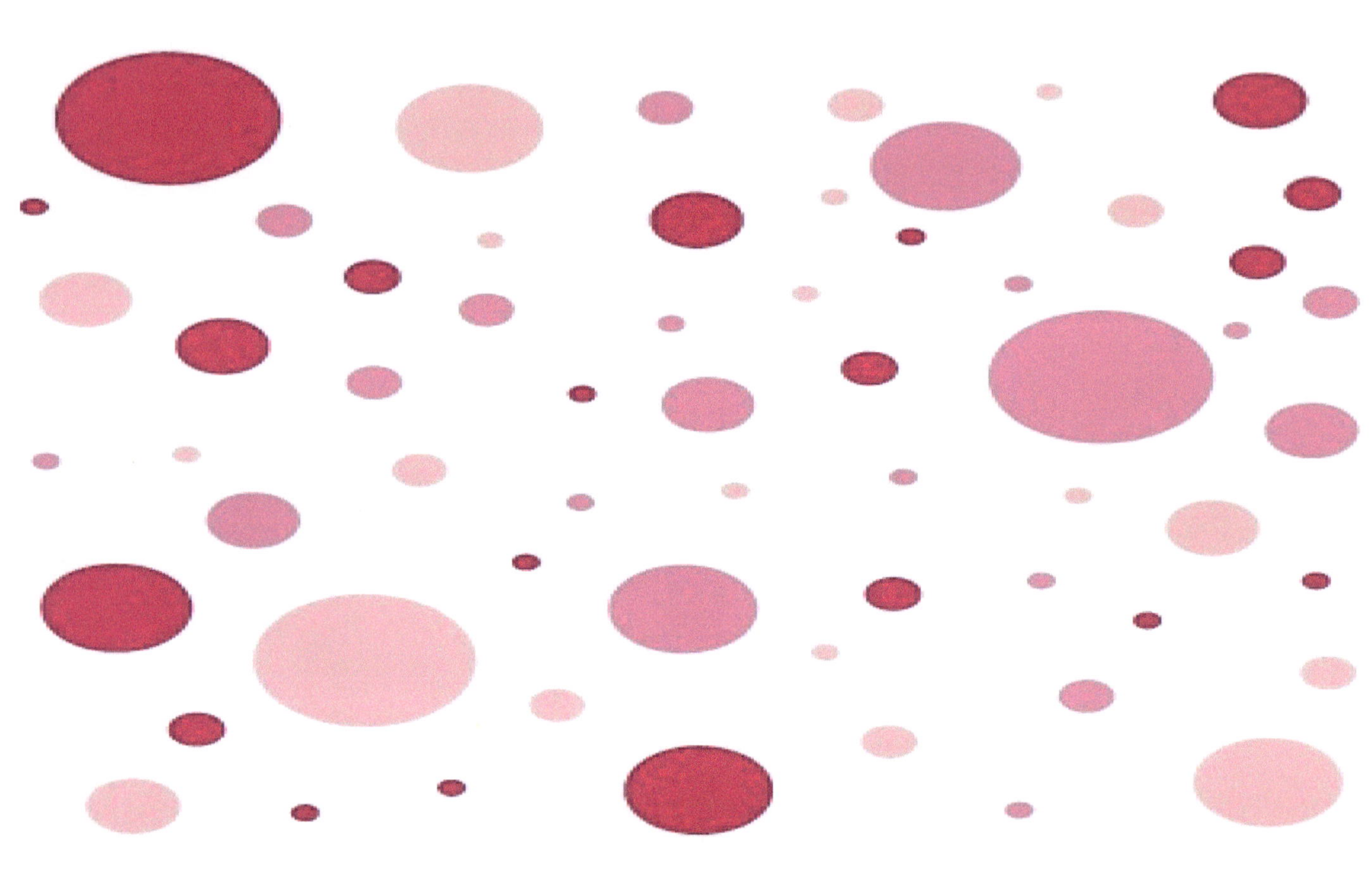

For all lovers of fruit bar popsicles, S.T.E.M, and Hip Hop, but especially our cousins, nieces, and nephews.

Ca'Myiah's Land is the place where life is lived authentically.
People are real. Even when we make mistakes we are allowed to
be true to our personality, spirit, and character.

No need to imitate a neighbor. For here, we find it cooler if we put to use the one thing or things that make us unique, special, and different.

In Ca'Myiah's Land everyone Hippity Hops to their own boogie down beat. The rhythm of their song is what makes life complete.

Hey, I am Ca'Myiah! My friends call me Mya or My.

This is my brother Davion, but family calls him "Juice" or "Dotte".

We are always with our cousin crew. Yes, it's me and "Dotte". Teagan who is both beautiful and fair. Little Xavier, but because he is so smart and excels at so many things, we just call him "X". And the quiet storm, Legend.

We love to make new friends. Cousins from birth. We are all the best of friends. Although tried, we remain true.

Everyday is an adventure. We never know what we will do. But as long as we are together in Ca'Myiah's Land, there is nothing we can't do.

We can write a rhyme. We can say a dope line. We have many fun ways to spend our time.

On the surface, are Hip hop moves look like we are just jumping around. Yet, we jump jovially. Because, we science kids, know we are just demonstrating the simplest form of quantum physics while simultaneously defying gravity.

Our math and coding skills are superb. We don't just step on those 1's and 2's. We also add, subtract, multiply, and divide them.

Whether we create, add, dance, sing, or play. Together we know we will have an Amazing Day! Hope to see you do what your great at too! Think of us as we do you! Maybe you'll come visit us in Ca'Myiah's Land real soon.

THE END.

Of this story,
but not of your Hip Hop and S.T.E.M.
journey.

Discussion Guide for Parents and Teachers

We all know that life can imitate art and art can imitate life. The author, trained as a Licensed Independent Mental Health Practitioner specializing in children and adolescent and expressive arts therapy. She hoped to create another safe place for children and children at heart to escape to while learning how to build or rebuild self-esteem one step or beat at a time. The author is inspiring a generation of minority children and girls to aspire to live their best life now which is the concept behind Ca'Myiah's Land. A place where everybody is somebody. Everyone is welcome. Everyone is special. Everyone is loved and celebrated. Where math, science and the arts can be seen in all things and appreciated by all is the best part of this book.

Credits

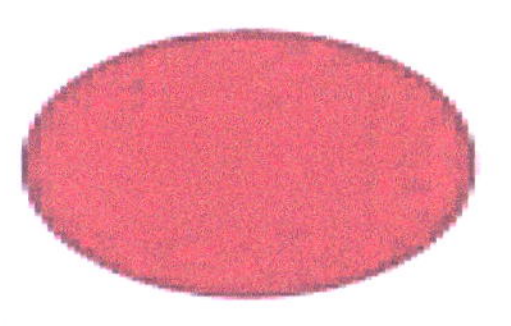

All images created and or adapted using the following free source pictures available at the following sites:
https:avanchara.com/childbaby
http:pncefranklin23.files.wordpress.com/2013/12/mus.jpg
http://clipart-library.com/clipart/qTBXpy49c.htm
http://moziru.com/images/road-clipart-yello-brick-road-6.png
https:openclipart.org
http://shevolution.uk.com
http://worldartsme.com
https://image.freepix.com
https;//wallpapercave.com/wp/UTOqrPb.jpg
Arts0551-2-16_0

Notes:

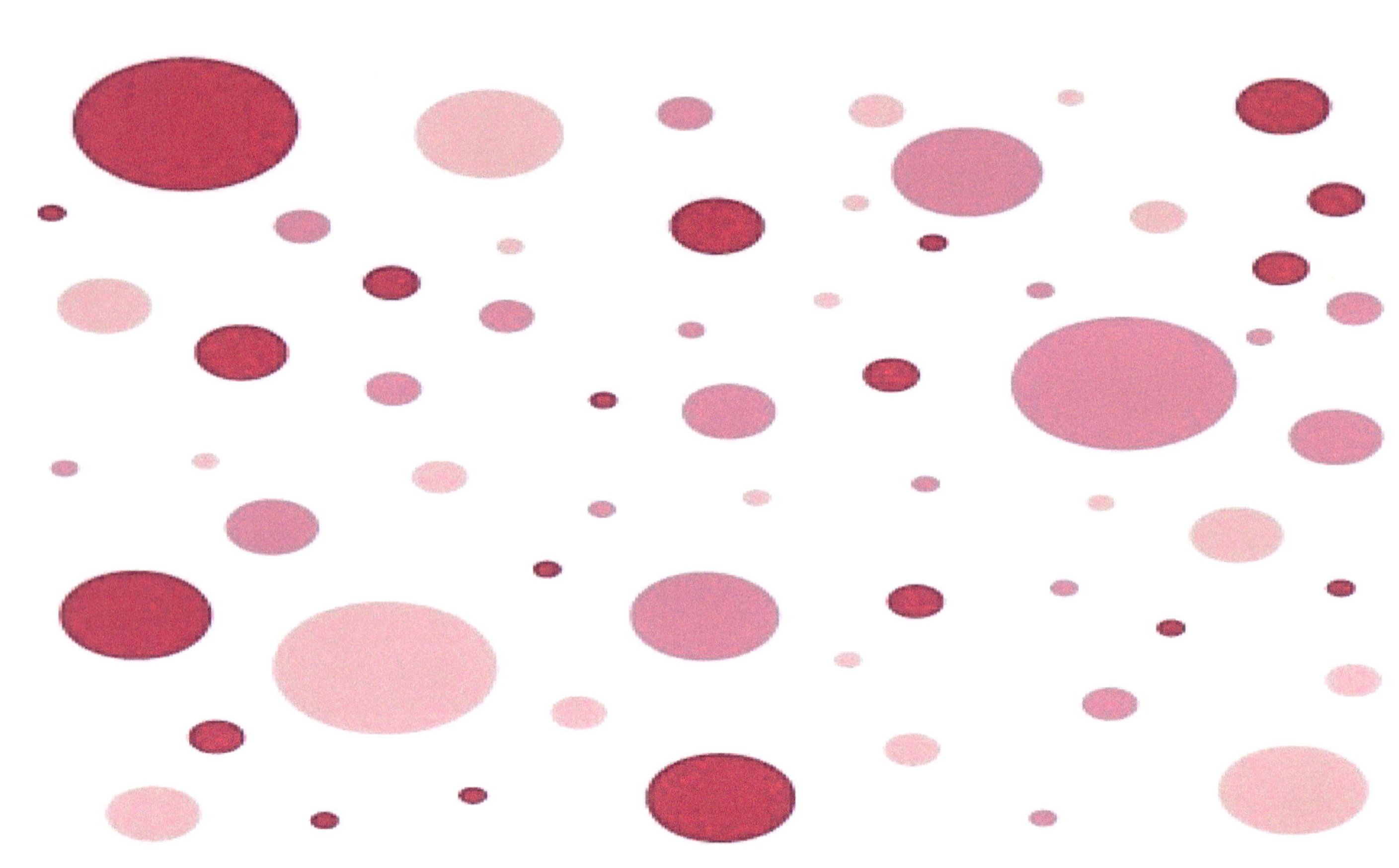

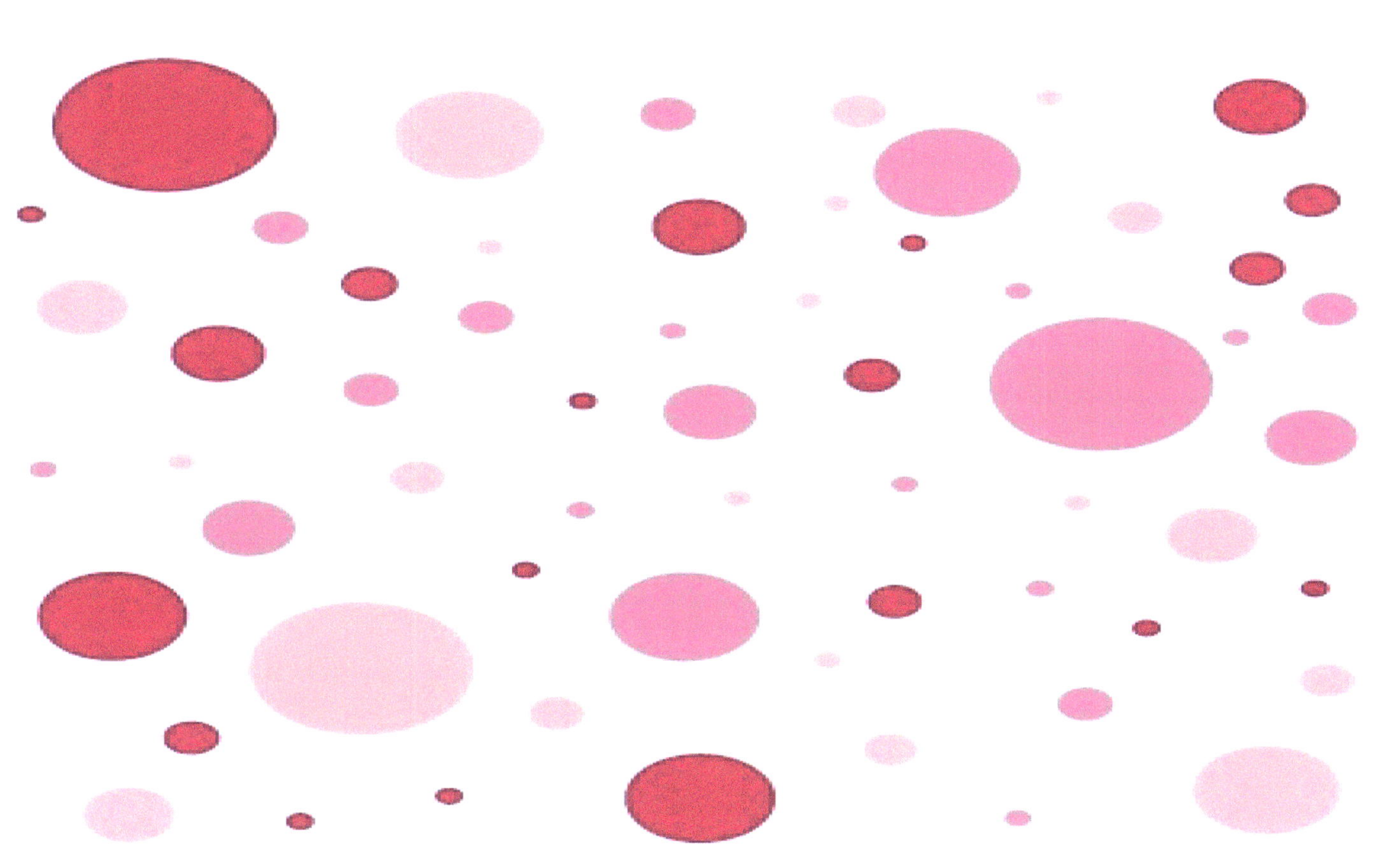